Pro

THOMAS MCCARTHY was born in Cappoquin, Co. Waterford, in 1954 and educated locally and at University College Cork where he was auditor of the English Literature Society. He has published many collections of poetry, including *The First Convention*, *The Sorrow Garden*, *Lost Province*, *Merchant Prince* and *The Last Geraldine Officer*. He has also published three novels, *Without Power*, *Asya* and *Christine* as well as two works of non-fiction, *Gardens of Remembrance* and *Out of the Ashes*. His *Pandemonium* was published by Carcanet Press in 2016 and was short-listed for the Irish Times/Poetry Now Award. He is a member of Aosdána, the Irish Assembly of artists and writers. He has won the Patrick Kavanagh Award, the Alice Hunt Bartlett Prize and the O'Shaughnessy Prize for Poetry as well as the Ireland Funds Annual Literary Award.

Prophecy

THOMAS McCARTHY

To Jay,
these poems of th Déese,
In Homage –
Tom N. C

July, 2019

CARCANET

First published in Great Britain in 2019 by
Carcanet
Alliance House, 30 Cross Street
Manchester M2 7AQ
www.carcanet.co.uk

MIX
Paper from
responsible sources
FSC® C014540

A CIP catalogue record for this book is
available from the British Library.
ISBN 978 1 78410 727 7

Book design by Andrew Latimer
Printed in Great Britain by SRP Ltd, Exeter, Devon

The publisher acknowledges financial
assistance from Arts Council England.

Supported using public funding by
ARTS COUNCIL
ENGLAND

Contents

for Mary Ahern

Prophecy

Bottling Shed, 1962

That afternoon Mnemosyne lay in dust
As her mother may or may not have foretold.
Who could trust Gaea after all the lust
Of nine consecutive steamy nights. So old

Was the world in the Walsh Hotel's back yard,
So full of memory was dust, that I was dead sure
Of disturbed geese and of fluttering Mass cards
Spilling together onto the hot street. Poor

As a church mouse was the world
After Zeus had gone back to Pieria. His
Nine daughters would scrub and scold
The universe of Green Street. You'd notice

Me, if you were interested, as the scarred
Domestic god helping Frank McLoughlin
To bottle warm beer from an amphora, a jar
As big as the two of us. Our bottling

In the old RIC barracks bottling-plant
Was as Greek and permanent as the warm
Build-up of a chorus, the apex of our duet sent
Into memory, full of malt, holding its form.

Toy Soldiers on a Window-sill

For what is spoken of, in general, is Goethe's
Gehalt, the import of things in any kind of poem,
As well as the images within. The scene
Of my childhood is more than a scene represented

And may not survive long enough
In the intellectual climate of our age,
This childhood window-sill where so much
Was tested. Yet not enough. Not adequate.

Soft metal soldiers of the Japanese armies
That came from Aunt Teresa in Houston,
An ambush heaven created by a paperback
Of Justice Warren's Kennedy *Commission*:

I tried not to look back. It was a paradox
To be so absorbed in my own battles. I could not
Withdraw my allegiance from inadequate truths,
Nor would I betray my troops. The window-sill

Was a battleground of condensation; the strife
In glass awaited clarification. Windows wept
If an ambush was confirmed or a soldier came to grief:
Such an enfilade of injury while the sirens slept!

And the strife behind me while I played –
Rainy Singapore fell in the heavy gun smoke
From my father's cigarettes. I tried
Not to breathe-in the surrenders he exhaled.

The Beginning of Colour

These brown discolorations on a faded black
And white photograph are not at all like a defect
In anything remembered, but, rather, a kind of
'crystalisation' as Stendhal described it, in
One of his more eccentric books about love.
In truth, my childhood was cast down like a twig
Into an abandoned salt-mine near Salzburg
From where it emerged, of this I'm certain,
As something much richer than my own life,
A jewelled branch of living history, now
Retrieved by my mother from the well at Twig
Bog Lane. I'll never know who it was, and anyway
Why would I want to know who it was
That slid the black hard plastic button to On
One late summer afternoon in nineteen fifty-seven,
So that not only did a kind of shutter flick open
In my head, but the full force of colour saturation
Hit my brain. The effect was high-speed Ektachrome
And life as it is now, that studio of constant poems –
It's just that as my mother hauled the metallic
Home Assistance milk gallon from the deep well
In Twig Bog Lane, the light of deprivation reflected
Back from her face and fell upon me, and I knew
How biography is the steadying of only one kind
Of lens, how memory offers different iterations;
How, somewhere, a paper was being coated with
Such chemicals that even deeper colours would form
Over time. During that summer, a world away,
The first International Colour Salon was organised

In Hong Kong and, while restrictions on dollar
Imports meant that Ireland couldn't reach a speed
Of 100 ASA, faster colours kept rushing in. There
Was no holding life back once it swarmed; biography
Was ready for colour, our brains were marked
That year for realities more personal, realities brighter
Than a boxed-in lens. Huge Blackwater river rats
That knawed through the doors of our dry toilets in
Twig Bog Lane were as ignorant of colour as me; and
Could not have known that their multi-layered bristles
Would soon be seen in more subtle shades of brown.

Ice Cream

That time in the long ago when my father said we are what we eat

He must have meant my Salvadorian light or the triple-
Shot slim latte that you so adroitly downed in three seconds flat.
If my memory serves me correctly it was three Raspberry Ripple
Ice-cream cones I'd consumed outside Fraher's old shop, bought
With money I'd earned for myself on the early morning news run.
But my idle father was not ready to cede authority, or not yet
Willing to abandon the upper-hand. He was fooling no one; even
Then I had no time for advice. Like my stomach, I was basically
Idle and middle-aged at the ripe old age of ten, maybe eleven.
Worst luck for me rather than him, but my hatred of authority
Would set me breaking windows inside my own stomach. It is not,
Let me repeat, it is never, a good thing not to listen to your father
Even if he's drinking lukewarm whiskey from a flask Dan Fraher
Gave him, even if his lung has begun its collapse into cigarettes.

Worse Than Nothing

Even then I knew that my life would be far less painful

Than my father had predicted. Cigarette poised
In a very superior gesture, a great gesture

Of idle, ill-deserved grandeur, he explained
That any effort I might make in Ireland

Would come to something worse than nothing.
It is this wet November drain I'm clearing of

Rotted leaves and cigarette-butts that puts
Him in my mind now – a beautiful cynic

For a father, a father who'd laugh at your dreams,
Who only loved that one Noel Coward song

'There Are Bad Times Just Around the Corner',
Not realising as I did, though a boy, that Noel Coward

Must have poked at many versions of that
Before the grey sludge moved, before the song came.

Rita Hayworth Sleeping

It must be the purpose of movies to make us fall in love –
She is pure quality and you were raised among grasshoppers
In a field of corn; a heart of gold, her eyes would be wide enough
To trap all the insects within. She may not be open to offers

Right now, but the lame excuses you give, the foolish way
You dance to Jerome Kern and Johnny Mercer's song
Even though you are still sitting, the rapturous sway
Of your soldier's body, convinces her that no dreadful wrong

Can come from this Private of the Southern Command
Who came to Dungarvan after the July Divisional exercise.
You are Fred Astaire taking Rita Hayworth's hand
Just as the moonlit dance begins and she closes her eyes –

My mother, I mean, then incredibly credulous and young,
Who would be fast asleep by the time they took to the floor,
Who would sleep right through whatever song was sung,
So that whether it was Ginger Rogers or Rita wanting more

My young mother would sleep and sleep. You were good,
My mother said, not to unbutton anything in her dreams,
But to wait for her waking report; to wait for her instead
To issue invitations, like a star. There is more than it seems

Always, and still more, when the reels turn behind you,
Making a sound like a swarm of grasshoppers on
A hot afternoon. Something trapped in her dancing shoe
Rises with you both, seeking light where the lights shone.

Falcons Hunting

Imperceptible disturbance there in the gloaming:

We raise our eyes to their ghostly presences,
A pair of falcons soaring above our windows –

See how steady they are in the air together,
Earth's most heavenly creatures taking the blue air

Of early June, as we are in the private hours
After Whitsun love-making. The crumpled

Sheets of feathery cloud, high as falcons,
Even higher, are love's unmistakable signature;

And these great high creatures, double nibs of life
Creating a single brushstroke, Chinese calligraphers

Of a long romance, just bank together
And sail into a fresh up-draft. The conjugal air

They recognise, I'm sure, the sudden, uncalled for uplift
That gives an even higher viewpoint. Such love

Between falcon and falcon is impossibly human.

I Love Also

The way birds in flight, bird motifs and fine drawings of birds
Draw you into their circle. It is as if there was something
In creatures of feathered flight, an improvisational air, a birdlike
Balancing act between the persistent patterns of wind and
The calculations of feathers, that responds to something
Not quite settled in you. I remember the owl at the hall door
Of old Parknasilla and how it spoke of you directly as if it knew
All the fiction you left hidden beneath stones from a time
When you were possessed with the migratory passions of
Youth. That owl had the dignity of George Bernard Shaw
And seemed to offer you a perch at the apex of a tall barn
In a fairytale. 'Meet me later and we'll catch some fat mice',
The owl seemed to be saying. 'Meet me later.' Today, it is
Tiny twittering song-birds hanging on for dear life in the
Catapult of fuschia branches in a force ten gale. They are,
You say, clinging in delicious fear like children on a fun-fair
Helter-skelter. They are born to this balancing act in a storm.

Wanting to Hold an Owl

Your wanting to hold an owl has developed feathers
Over the years so that now your idea or desire
Is something that could take to the night sky with
All the quiet wingspan of a human being in love
With wings and with the wings' impossible yearning
To be a spirit with an uncontrollable fire
Like a hunter without words, as the predator in
The thing you desire has called your name over
And over in a book on a shelf years and year ago –
It must be the night sky that can hold so much
Of what we might desire, so that the ink in the thing
We can't see from Adam, ink of our night, is Eve's
Desire to hold, just for a little while, the one long
Extended feather of the night; the wide eyes, the bird
And its certainties, the immense power of its quiet.

Figs at Aghios Nikolaos

Sometimes you say that only the Greeks understood love,
You must mean love in the purest sense of the word, and not

Matrimony or rebirthing so much as the very lust itself –
It is not the cradle at the end of a contract, you say, not
The lust that fades into a generation hence, but pity of

A kind lived to the end of a singular life, the pitiful
Golden amber of enclosed yearnings; and possession like

Loss, so much like loss that nothing else is left to say
In a marvellous contract between a love and a love. Then

You must mean a love like figs, I suggest, these early figs
Of August that have bloomed into a soft purple heart of

Themselves alone. I press into them, giving and delicate,
And I place my tongue where an exhausted wasp once

Left an impression of frail wings, wings of a yearning life
That had desire only in its passing, a fig-wasp's one desire.

Son, Husband, Father

for Catherine

Naturally, I thought all men were rubbish until life
Proved otherwise. Here I would like to write about
Other roles for men, but this woman who agreed to be my wife
Is sharpening the blades of the hedge-trimmer. I pout
By the box-hedge while she grinds steel to a cutting gleam.
I wish I knew how to do that, but she came into her own
As a thrower of knives in a prison art room; and she seemed
To have skills beyond her years. What was thrown

At all comers was her genius for wrist technique.
That she wasn't interested in gender while I was interested
In how to be a man explains my current pique
As well as my pique over the years. 'I am done and dusted
With margins,' she said, 'And you are not to think
Of me as a feminist knife-thrower. Why does everything
Women do need to have some kind of gender dynamic?'
I thought of my own soufflé on the rise and my nurturing

Nature; and the way I had ironed her best white shirt.
Her own nature leapt off the page at our very first meeting
And I was hooked, or was I pinned? When at first
She said I was a strange son who needed hard editing
I didn't know then that she'd make me a father. Here
She comes now, with rasp and file, washers and easing oil:
Husband-maker, father-maker. I hand her a cold beer
And a thing I fixed earlier, a paean from the slush-pile.

Cats on the Rampart

We lie here in the Calle Vallaresso,
Atop the golden orb of its irreconcilable
Antimonies, listening to the B-side
Of Italy as it plucks at the heart strings
Of tourism. This is cheap: as Venice
Goes, more a sketch of the experience
Of being in a hotel than any Palazzo
Upon a lagoon. The thumping sound
Of Nick Cave's 'Opium Tea' is as
Incongruous as the neurasthenic
Tiredness of our Venetian summer,
Its insistent yearning a tincture of
Consonants among suicidal vowels,
Its deadly ennui scoring the night's
Preparatory canvas. Tom-cats of the
Innkeeper's niece have been howl-
ing for hours, but your Bluetooth gondola
Has kept us afloat. We have brought
Ourselves and our contradictions to a
Perfect bedroom. We could have stayed
At home, but that would have been
To miss the point. It is Italian cats,
con brio, who build a bridge of sighs.

Sing the Shehecheyana

I arrive this particular day in plumes of adult breath,
My rib-cage still working the bellows.
Here on this new jetty in Dingle town I can see
Jacob wrestling with the angel of history. Here's

A small harbour, a simple gratitude that I've lived
To see an arrangement of such nets and fish;
And the body within me
That turns like a sail in a cross-wind

To face the light –
It's just that I've lived to see this particular day
And you turn to me like a Jewish girl from my youth
As we lift together this sacred scroll

To sing as one of our simple gratitude.
It was Yehuda Amichai, once, do you remember,
On a roof in Old Jerusalem?
If our long relationship now seems a miracle it is

Because days advance to our Torah portion,
Making a game attempt to master the
Cantillation marks, deciding which part of this hour
Goes with this tune in my head, this watermark.

There Once Was a Girl

After tea and toast in this railway-junction café
I begin another session in the workshop of my life.
I begin as always with a memory of humiliation:
Something small enough, you see, or something
Distant but flickering still like the red tilly lamp
Lighting the last coach of a train I may have missed;
Something to illuminate the day more memorably
So that it leaves an impression, a leaf of time
Pressed against my skin, some arrangement of veins
And lines in the morning's afterthought. The fact is
I don't have an open ticket, but my mind still
Believes that I can catch any train that I want. It
Would pain me to think otherwise. But the facts are
Otherwise. Otherwise, surely, I'd have taken a train
Earlier, I'd not have risked life leaving me behind
In this café in a poem. It is true that thinking thus
Is a generative exercise; that this session in a café
Of waiting, a place of name-calling and destinations
Where knives and forks are polished silver and the
Staff are trained and gracious, that this space
In a poem may also feel otherwise. All this
Metaphor and trauma and formal technique
I place in my canvas travel bag. And as I rise
From my chair it is a girl I knew once who clings
To the session I've made at this breakfast table,
A girlfriend who said she desired a much older man;
That he touched her in a way I knew nothing about,
That she loved him and it couldn't be otherwise.

As Blue

I have almost nothing left to say about agapanthus and *Scilla siberica*,
Except for the blue. I mean the blue hue that they offer us, as if blue
Was the best they could do. Blue is a code if you're from Waterford;
Or not a code, more a chord. It is the music of blue I hear. What's new
Is not new, not really, but it is certainly as fresh as Antarctica
Every winter as they both fight off neglect to find a folk memory
Like a snatch of song by Labhrás O Cadhla or Nioclás Tóibín, the two
Of them fighting it out like women of the Connerys; or that tailor
Who eloped with a beautiful girl, such folk memory that reaches me
Here by a brick wall where agapanthus wants to forget an old blue
And become an insipid white from the root. What are flowers for
Except to obey us? There will be no turning away from blue, I can
Tell you, no turning away at all. As always, I have strong women to
Guide me. There will be no turning away such women, though I admit
That Mrs C.W. Earle liked the white campanulata in a large pan
Of saxifrage, with, instead of holes, sharp crocks where bulbs might sit –
I hope she wasn't referring to her husband who'd by now be blue
In the face from all the correcting impulses of his gifted wife. As
For Mrs Jekyll, who loved the charms of dog's tooth violet, she saw
A suspicion of green beneath blue's other penetrating qualities. True,
She loved the rarity of that rare blue. She wouldn't lay down any law
Against scilla though, seeing blue in her woods as a memory of blue.

After Surgery

As I was saying, before the news became
Really bad, as I was saying, we hardly know
What it is to breathe. Whether it is being
Distracted or being in a constant state of
Fear, we forget the immense gratitude
That our lungs still function. Or maybe by
Breath I mean something more than air,
More how a feeling of separation vanishes
When we exercise awareness rather than
Self-torture. It is the proper function of
Poets to make us want to breathe. Love makes
Long words out of the simplest emotion –
We weave in its backdrafts and elongations,
We twist and turn, we live and we grasp.
I remember in Mercy hospital the young
Croatian anaesthetist saying gently as
She pulled on a tube 'I think you can breathe
On your own now, you are doing so well.'
The annoyance of being cut adrift! But my
Lungs pulled away from the shore on their
Own, my lungs pulled and pulled on what
Was needed for breath. The surgical ward
Fell away in its own Vipassana meditation,
Its ego was eradicated and a sort of mind
That was like a mind of mindfulness just
Filled the whole room and a companionship
Like the companionship of Buddha and his
Holy disciples carried me back to my own life,
Away from an inert physics and medicine;

Back, back to what is personal and full of blood.
The Buddha was a troublemaker in his own
Time but he never caved in at a cancer ward, or
Succumbed to the epidural or to any horror
Of laziness or distracted mind. My true breath
Is this feeling of having just arrived, of sturdy
Essences, of breath going on by going through.
And yet this really bad news, can it be true,
Of Leonard Cohen's death in a faraway place,
Has made me think of breath again, of love's
Survival, of Suzanne and Marianne, of Leonard
Sleeping in Yeats's bedroom at Lissadell. They say
He slept alone, with only bats stirring in the alcoves
Of an Irish night. Such news has been bad lately, but
We must fight the empty void, the out of breath.

Second Night

A dead deer on the road to the surgical ward,
A deer that mis-timed a leap the way

I mis-timed this encounter. I break cover
The way an animal does and I escape

Into the lair of a Mercy Hospital bathroom.
It is the sourness that shatters me. I am

As sour, momentarily, as my father was sour
When you mentioned a name. Any name –

To be a name in life was to be a disappointment.
What this cancer tells me, to be honest,

Is how we are all unknowable, how when
The chips are down you are supremely on your

Own and as supreme as any maker. For
You have conjured a something out of a nothing

And the years that compress themselves
Against the cold wall of a hospital when

You are on your own in the dead of night
Are brilliant with compressions. Lights in

The corridor are really the nurses flying past,
And specks of dust that the cleaners

Will catch tomorrow are as wayward as the DNA
That mutated into an event in my optimism.

It is the carcass of a deer on the side of a road
And its understanding of heaven that keeps

Me awake. Too early for a thing as banal as pain,
I've been almost not optimistic for two days.

Age and Creativity

I'm not old enough to be truly aged but I can see age
Before me, today, at this Aosdána lunch, age in all
Its complicated shuffles and hesitations, its heritage
Of folding back upon itself to compress the hard crystal

Of hours that once were loose and loosely scattered.
Life will become a field hospital of the Great War
For all of us who are lucky to survive. Our shattered
Minds will be no worse than the Verey lights and gore

Of a pointless advance through mud. Here is a poet,
Infirm as Robert Graves, who wills me to replenish
His empty water glass. The bucket where ice cubes float
Is beyond his reach. Even the cold in water seems to perish

When you are too old to move quickly. But his mind
Is sharp and quick as a Sergeant Major's, his bark
Is the command of poems published before my time.
I bring him comfort from the Moss Depot and park

My arse where I can listen and learn, his two
Baby Powers in a coffee cup. Waiters are busy as
Tunnellers behind enemy lines, wanting to shoo
Us quickly away, but I am like the captain at Arras

Who has heard a shot while reading Masefield's
Delicate poems, knowing someone has found death
In a shallow dugout, yet hesitant behind shields
Of earth and wood, unwilling to advance just yet.

Louise Bourgeois, Patrick Pye

The repair of a tapestry or a costume is precisely a plea in favour of a second chance.

— *Louise Bourgeois, 29 October 1995*

There are compelling reasons why we must stay alive longer;
And not just to fulfil the commentary of Edward Said or Gottfried
Benn. The angst and depth of life, healing when we misremember,
Or writing as therapy in the strict therapeutic sense; yes, we need

All of these meanings, but I think it is really that there's a spider
With a vast bronze maternity who hovers over its own bronze eggs
To teach us a lesson about endurance. Youth may be a mother
But it only gives birth to the first things. A motherhood of dregs

Is what old age gives birth to, a protective leather of artifice, a soul
Double-distilled, completely mediated by time. Let us go back,
As Louise Bourgeois does, to an installation of life as a whole,
To the long calm settled story of the self. What old age may lack

In promise it more than fulfils in half-worn materials, in costumes
Of memory appliqued over and over. I wish to live my life perpetually
Which is why I need this second chance to heal. These fumes
From the recovery room are a perfume. I can't move but I can see

Other humans moving among the living on this ledge; and as I
Return to this one world of compulsions and imperatives old
Threads tighten and medicine restores a terrain level with my eye.
I look out again. I construct a late life on foundations that are cold

But getting warmer. I am transported. I am not stone. Such words
As come to me make a childhood that art has swallowed whole.
Rain lashes frail gurneys and drips, lightning flashes in surgical wards,
Making a bronze material of my misfortune. This running down of

The human machine is full of whim and pathos, as delicate, even,
As a handkerchief-tree in a storm. Such vulnerability of love
As the old feel is nothing more than that style, or, as Linda Nochlin
Calls it in her Bourgeois essay, 'Old-Age Style', a late harvest

Without any guarantee of moral superiority, along with a trembling
Hand or a fumbling brushstroke. Or, age may be an interfering pest,
A meddler with every possibility of closure – age as a mad King –
Though misfortune yearns for an elegiac climax, an Indian Summer

Of general colour and local tones. Barely awake and breathing
When someone in a blue gown bends over me and begins to sing,
I give birth to thoughts and constructs. I sing to the young singer. I
Must go on in an artful way. I feel as immortal as Patrick Pye.

In 1974

Northerly on our island, beyond the hybrid daffodils,
The rare ones bought from Richard Hartland in Cork
And soon flourishing like native things, in a part
Of Ireland far from where a guerrilla unit had killed,
Adroitly killed, a young mother in her mobile home,
Leaving two bullet marks in her daughter's stuffed
Kermit frog: beyond that bustling April drawing-room
There was still history's twilight zone. Not enough
Dying had been done, in our public way I mean,
To satiate the arguments, or to quiet the insufferable
Holy past. I was Josephus, for sure, hating trouble
And its plural and capitalised iteration and all unseen
Carriers of death who've brought nothing but
Misery into our written record. A watercolour
Sky, a primed canvas always wanting more
Of texture and conversation, another dark exhibit,
Embraced this gathering of aging men. A Golgotha
Was called for, or a pardidomi, a handing over
Of some kind of truth in the quality of this Passover
In Irish history. I was looking elsewhere for prophecy, a
Mark or Luke I might kiss in recognition, a Synoptic
Lullaby. Instead, in this poem, I hand over to Pontius Pilate
One navigator of the RAF, one commander of a frigate,
A liaison officer of Belgian lifelines, a Brigadier Mick –
I felt so close to England at that moment I could hear
Sirens and the smell of two industrialised wars. Sherry
And daffodils did comfort this gathering, their memories
So like my own, still yearning for an epoch to be over.

Remembrance Day

Here is an ageing Colonel between marble and trees
Reading the story of a wood

That was pulverised
In the name of any number of small nations

The way something big can pulverise what's
Small in the name of a huge thing.

It is not huge, history.
Astonishing, how intimate. At the sound

Of his assured story-telling

Poppies and wildflowers lean into the camera,
A guardsman is rigid as the dead,

I mean the dead seeming as dead as Walter Barron
Of Co. Waterford and the other dead

Listening for something like this voice,
This one haunting story. Please, sir, tell us again.

Our Irish Anniversaries, 2016

I

An Enthusiasm

I clamour to enlist in history. Nothing
In Ireland should happen without me, no
Ambush or artwork, no new hospital built
Or social home. I bring an old mattress
To the barricades, I bring abandoned poems;
I bring boiled potatoes, still hot inside green
Wrappings of an old *Irish Press*. I place
Blessed candles in all the windows of our old
Cottage to light Daniel O'Connell home.

II

A Counter-Enthusiasm

I love as much that long dissent from what
I love: Bill Allen's enthusiasm, for example,
When he stood up in the House as an Ulster MP
To propose a tunnel under the independent Irish
That would integrate the entire NI and GB –
A dream that died with the fate of railways;
And yet his intent as old as Londonderry, as
Ancient as Ulster dissent. For we are never what we
Describe, but we are always what we seem.

Garden of Remembrance

I

These stones report for duty in story after story,
The garden a cistern of unsweetened water;
Time's patina burnished by an effort to remember,
Such effort renewed at each national anniversary
Where sea-gulls glide over the field of slaughter
To uncover another trail of poems. Time is a hoarder
That gathers us together behind the box hedge
To remember glory, to define a lost cause
Or a cause renewed at the hour of remembrance.
We remember our prayers and the seagull's rage,
So careful now – now so conscious of the past –
That we may not create yet more victims. What lasts
In a Republic is the living and so in this age
I remember the living on this cold, grassy ledge.

II

Our remembrance is a form of theatre, as each
Remembrance is, in every nation. An eternal flame
Burns elsewhere and cenotaphs hold heroic names;
Remnants of us pepper each Normandy beach
And poppies grow up out of our bones. But here
I think of the one nation the poets imagined
And think again of the two states we're in,
A state of mystical borders and broken spears
Left by a silent procession of things left unsaid.

It's not that our cowardice has deepened; or not
Cowardice, not that, but an indifference yet
Unchallenged, an indifference to the innocent dead
That creeps along the wall of memory, as moss
Or ivy muffle traffic noise or mask all heroic loss.

III

A shuffle of wet tiles, history's lovely aquamarine –
All the weapons lie abandoned after battle
Like the leaves of Sessile oak, *Dair Ghaelach*,
That scatter in a sudden burst of wind. We seem
Drawn to history, fatally, the way troubled
Families want to pace across the same old ground
In the hope of comfort from what comes round.
I find an empty bench where history doubled
Back and came to life in a fantasia of warm metal;
Oisín Kelly's mythic swan children now seem
Like children abandoned in refugee-camp or great famine,
Arms hanging loosely in great bronze petals –
After all the Troubles, politics wants to make peace
With art, but memory is immovable in a stiff breeze.

IV

James Connolly's beautiful life, the high aesthetic
Of Pearse, the gift of three buttons from Con Colbert's
Volunteer uniform, Thomas MacDonagh's verse –
Listen, in this remembering place I pick
Strange names to add to the forgotten dead:

Willie Redmond explaining how at the Ulster line
In front of Ploegstreet the Southerners arrived
And words of love between two Irelands were said
Before slaughter swallowed the young. And Harold
Mooney of the RAMC, his shattered left thigh,
Should remind us of how the unsung are left to die
In a free state of dying slowly. All their untold
Stories haunt me still. Permit me to remember the dead
On the wrong side of revolution, the part they played.

v

Mothers from another continent come here to rest.
Memory is a kind of cradle. Memory is a giant beech
In a sunlit meadow. I watch a new migrant child reach
Into this restored reflecting-pool, his outline traced
In a cruciform pool of disturbed shadows. What can he know,
This child of worldly exile, of the purpose
Of this city-centre park? How can you or I propose
A better Ireland, a safer shelter in the quiet meadow?
Here in this Irish world, in the last place where God
Found us useful, we have a duty to make a nest –
Not an ill-advised pageant or a national barricade.
When the midday sun breaks through, my eyes rest
On harp and acorn, on trumpet and bronze hands,
On things a family without our history understands.

Rebellion

My betters have died for Ireland but I prefer to remember
Chiffon, I mean the sheer black chiffon gown that followed

Ginger Rogers in the perfect revolution of her body, that time
When she ambushed an orchestra. It was her commandante

In white tie and tails, that task master and patriot
Fred Astaire, who turned and turned as if bullets

Were heat-seeking and meant for him. But Ginger
In her folds and folds of shimmering black

Outclassed everything low calibre, rising like a statue
Of some outdated deity turning to molten lead

And spilling across the dance-floor with entire nations
Looking on. It should be just for this that young boys die.

With my betters looking on, I still wish to choose chiffon;
Perhaps because I am a poor mother's son, working-

Class and politically ignorant. I mean I might have
Fought in a Great War, without my national interests at heart,

Only to come home to this, this one consolation of chiffon
In a dance-hall where we met, in a post-war dance routine.

Field Hospital, 1917

Love, though I am trying to dump when my bowels won't move
I'm still proud to have lost a limb for Ireland. It is not too bad

To lose just an arm. There were never any guarantees, as Mr
Redmond said that night in Waterford. No point being sad

When your number's up. Shrapnel burst low over the fire-bay,
My flesh became clay. I was wearing a woman's white undergarment

As camouflage in snow. Frost and *minenwerfers*, the grand scream
Of shells in a blizzard: Tommy Mason, Walter Barron, Cappoquin men,

All gone down. Are we paying too high a price for this Parliament
Of our own? Home is so personal when you're in pain,

It seems ghoulish to want a nation. I moan and think how you
Looked in your Jubilee Nurse uniform. I may have lost an arm,

Waterford woman, but I still want an armful of you. Now this
Auxiliary nurse from Carlyle checks my pulse and says 'Well

Done, well done.' With chloroform I can't do a thing. I can only
Make fart-smells and not a real dumping. A smell is no good

For an artillery man, a smell is always too political. Yesterday, there was
Captain Keane of the Big House, and one Coughlin, the farmer's son.

Now, a Mr Ussher's nephew in the Munster Fusiliers
Has come with a little book of Irish words, words such as '*botúin*'

And '*ár*', those simpler Irish words for unquantifiable
Things. I mean the word for 'error' and the word for 'slaughter'.

The Passing of Old Ukraine

in memory of W.E.D. Allen

It was when they took control of Kerch
And Yenikale, of the Don basin, the Azov Sea,
That you became more than an intellectual Ulster
Unionist, more than a Sech from a little country –

You saw how loyalty can be removed from its silver
Frame, quite easily; and how people flee
From history, dropping icons at the far side of the river.
The bravery of the Hetmans, the insolence of poetry,

It always ends in something far less spectacular –
The way Ulster settled in your unsettled mind
And became nothing like what Prince Potemkin dreamed
For a borderland. New dissensions always arise

With unfinished business, though hatred always needs
A constant blood supply. Let us build an ephemeral
Architecture, let's deceive the peasantry with theatrical
Effects: make of the future a painted dream.

You wrote furiously, describing each New Russian scene
As if history were happening for the first time,
Though it was only a chapter, a new iteration
In the formal tedium of war. Not King Billy

This time, but Bily, who received the heroic
Standard – a blue cross on a white field:
Ten million hectares redistributed, a little
More than two kopecks per acre; and blessed

Relief for Gritsko the Dishevelled. There was ferment
Among the grim Tartars, trouble in the Steppe;
Yet imperial beneficence seemed heaven-sent,
The way you described it: such caviar and drink

As victors always have. Still, even now I can't think
How you, dear Ulsterman, pencilled every detail in –
Marvelling, in prose, at the way fleeing Cossacks dropped
Their honey bees, or whether Balmoral had roses still.

A Don Cossack by the Sea of Marmara

History may be a misfortune, but it's no accident:
I listen to this lost and crippled Caucasian troubadour
Singing songs of an unreliable regiment – a regiment
Of camp-followers rather than soldiers. I can gather
From his wailing ballads and the hardy wooden leg
That remnants of war are pathetic still, that any
War worth its weight in salt will leave a lyric of wounds,
As wars tumbled over our own land in a bitter effort
To cause songs, indeed not only songs but a history
With a feel for music that could claim dominion over
All future war; I mean the moral rights left behind
By injury; I mean the right to remember lyrically in
This way and in that way, keeping all sides at the war
In the hope of a chorus. It is complex, this music. It is
More than a boy with a mouth-organ; even more, I
Would say, than any man with a printing-press and a
A feel for songs. We are all most angry with the near
Abroad. Music is the prince of borderlands who leads
Us on, songs to mark the site of ambush, songs where
The others' treachery is exposed. As I was saying, as
This troubadour carried on, you'd give away a small
Country for a really good song, you would, don't lie,
You'd kill for a harp or a sash, you would: I know
Your musical kind, you'd kill, you'd kill and not think
Of anything but the song in your head at the moment
Of killing, I tell you, you'd rush the nearest borderland
To clear it of all others to make it pure. You would. You
Bloody well, you. You well blood-soaked, you would
Tumble away from where the last device exploded.

You would, you would bring the other to his knees
With ease, you would, you would. A poor troubadour,
Legless from war, is recruiting already by this hidden
Sea. It is the salt of wounds all the way to Basra, it is
A great desert where Turkish divisions regroup, it is a
Caucasian tree-line where guerrillas muster behind icons.
It is a song, and more than a poem, where patriots
Rush to reassemble. Blame the song, soldier, because
It is not that some ill-advised parliament or drunken
Monarch has placed you in exile so far from the Don,
But a delicate Ulster scholar, a Mr W.E.D. Allen of West
Belfast, who wrote you into his narrative as a small
Turkish footnote, a bother; a bleak Russian addendum.

How It's Going to Play Out

for Dervla Murphy

None of us are sure how it's going to play out
For America and none of us, in this Irish pub,
Want to be around at the hanging. We are a hub
Of misery ourselves; and sometimes our clout –

Our only clout in the whole world – was complaint.
We are good at this, having had much to complain
About; you know, the Tudor Plantations and Great Famine
And all that, as well as various forms of restraint

By hostile British parliaments down the years,
From the Cattle Acts of 1660, the Penal Laws,
The laws that destroyed Irish woollens; the cause
After cause that became one Great Cause

By which our feral hatred of England was born.
Now that we've been passing through an unlikely calm
For years, and susceptible once more to English charm,
We can see the logic of Imperial interests, the forms

Of possessiveness that discoveries brought; the sheer
Unstoppable impulses of expansion and trade:
We are less Roger Casement and more Joseph Conrad.
Yet, we are still comfortable with this Battle of Algiers

That's just been shown after the nil-nil FIFA game.
In this pub we recognise the text and the subtext,
As easily as we understood the film on Malcolm X
Last week, and Costa Gavras's *Z* and the theme

Of *Missing*, so like *In the Name of the Father*.
It's just that counter-terrorism can't be as precise
As the police work in *Der Baader Meinhof Komplex*,
Nor as precisely executed. I could go farther

Than I need to go, but you know precisely what I mean –
It's not the first outrage but counter-terror that makes poetry
And what we fear in this pub, as we down our fourth whiskey,
Are the poets beneath hoods, and terror becoming poems.

The Dead of Albuera

Let them play
Their game of lives, and barter breath for fame:
Fame that will scarce re-animate their clay,
Though thousands fall to deck some single name.
— Byron, 'Childe Harold's Pilgrimage', Canto the First, XLIII

'We have made love. All night in Ezra's bed
My girl and I made love,' Desmond O'Grady said,
'It was a Byronic and Venetian ecstasy
For which my lovely companion deserves a PhD.'

I was at that very moment, like Alessandro
Gentili and John Montague, dying of thirst
And unable to walk to the pub in heavy snow,
Though enchanted by Byron's Canto the First

And angry at the dead of Albuera –
That Olga Rudge gave our Munster poet a bed
Was no less incongruous than the dead,
The thousands dead, of a bloody Peninsula

That stamped the wrinkles deeper
On the brow of a worn-out poet.
Literature as a fragment was popular
When the slaughter of men was not

A thing universally regretted: we make
Love to see those fragments cohere. We
Are preoccupied, make no mistake,
By life's great emptiness. You see,

You must see, the meaning of Ezra Pound's
Welcoming bed: all the Venetian stars
Glowed in Desmond's call, though the sound
Heard in Cork was of an older, Byronic war.

George Boole

Wealth consists of things transferable, limited in supply, and either productive of pleasure or preventive of pain

— *Senior*

$$w = st\{p(1 - r) + r(1 - p)\}$$

— *Boole*

Dust and autumn has come to the Boole Assembly Area
And leaves perform the ritualistic algebra
Of assembling in parentheses of October red.
I sit with my back to the world, being sixty
Years old in a Quad colonised by the young –
Though the young have been young indefinitely, it could
Be said; and only the trees grow old like me
In what was once Queen's College, now autumnal UCC.

Here George Boole, like the young, can't become old
But is perpetually stirred by abstractions of air
And by this world of constant graduations. Time is sold
More than once. Time is sold over and over
In a pedagogy of diaphanous veils and the spare
Liquid fluency of hours; in leaves that hover
A moment in a puff of post-graduate wind,
Leaves that come to rest like an equation in a mind

That seemed settled before the exercise began. Now
Is the hour of mathematics: our mindful presence is logical
Like the on-off switch of pure knowledge. How
Can we ever know what our first professor knew

Of all the laws of thought? What was Greek became algebraic
Inside his head; and human fate became renewable.

I turn in awe, for I am now in love with the angled atrium
Inside Boole Q+3; books and data that dispel the gloom.

North of Duluth

in memory of Roger Blakely

We're back down to grey highways of buckled heat,
Back from the high-bush cranberry cool
Of our one Heartbreak Creek
Or homely Shovel Point in its hawkish zig-zag

Of shattered spruce. Lake water of sapphire and mirrors:
We cannot accept the inevitable miles.
Boulders and scragwood make way, and summer
Like the very fine bones of grilled pike

Is stuck in our throats. Not a word between us,
But the fear of a new school year. We shall never taste
The scarlet maple now or the Nordic wind
Driving south in Canadian bitterness. Our minds

Are still freakish with summer, and incapable of friends.
What whirrs between us in late August heat
Is nothing less than thunder and sky – except for this:
A mysterious girl hitch-hiking in the middle of nowhere,

Breaking the skyline with her canvas bag and violin case.
Oh, you must mean Roger Blakely or John
Bernstein if you're coming south
To study at Macalester. Not that she wished to give away

Too much as we moved deeper and deeper south:
You could follow the cedar waxwing, or you could,
She said, hang out with Schubert. I knew then she must be
A Nordholm or Helberg, a Becklund or Lindstrom.

Counter-Mannerism and Early Baroque

If what I love is my true inheritance then I inherit this
Tremendous counter-point, our two lives running parallel
On a quiet Sunday before the year folds into Christmas,
Before we contemplate together Matteo Rosselli's 'St Paul

In Damascus', or this truly divine canvas of the Archangel
Michael looking like a pampered youth of Florence
With his mysterious grin. There's half of Italy in this catalogue
Where Matteo rests, now, for ten thousand Euro –

As if a door to love could be bought that cheaply. It is,
Quite simply, a cathedral, this love; it is entered on tiptoe
Like the cloister of the Basilica della Santissima Annunziata
Or an 'Adoration of the Magi' at the church of Montevarchi.

On tiptoe I reject these distortions of High Mannerism,
And I refute, absolutely, any partial return to God
That art might promise in its chiaroscuro and charisms.
But something of Rosselli's simplicity, his grey mood

In plain tunic, his simple buttons, what looks like an unstarched
Collar – so strange in Florence – and a statement, perhaps,
Of the simple heart of an artisan; something of his rich
Clarity reaches us across the centuries. Love escapes

From its Roman mannerism to declare itself, so that as we sprint
Like exiles of the Waldense across the marbled endpaper
Of the year, we see the parallels between art and attachment –
How such an art declares love's clarity, and its formal order.

Reading *American Song* by Paul Engle and *The Land* by Vita Sackville-West

A poet becomes inexorably minor. It was
Something that agitated tall Louis McNeice –
Antrim's best poet by a mile – as he wove
A beautiful life out of complex poems, yet
Felt wet and discommoded from that
Constant heavy rain of a cloud called Auden.
And poor Theodore Roethke, remember
Him? So major was Roethke among weeds
And florists he felt briefly aggrieved with
You and your own Iowan 'salt of the earth';
With how you charmed all of Oxford, how
You rowed in a Merton crew, how you
Came home to a front-page *New York*
Times review. He struggled, Paul Engle, with
A poet-professor's burden of being obscure
In a land of so much nourishment, in fields
With a hard certainty of harvest – as the
Beautiful Vita Sackville-West struggled
To come to terms with a poetry beyond
Towers and trees. How could chopped-up
Prose mean what true verse means? How
Could a waste land be better than Sackville
Gardens and noble poems? If we allow
Everything common in, God forbid, how will
What is beautiful survive? O, Vita,
Not everything loved can be a Violet; nor
Can love be complex for every poet, a
Golden bird in a gilded cage, a chorister
In a deep wood, or a husband told that

He may never break through the way you
Do. Ah, you had more than a full plate
And yet it was your own *The Land* broke through
Into middle-class fame, all twenty thousand
Copies then swept away by an urgent war –
So that as we travel all the way back to where
Your name became obscure we find ourselves
Truly in a place of horror, a place where death
And reputations become sexless things; a kind
Of tomb where an indifferent sun settles
With less light than warmth. Briefly, in Iowa.

Thigh-Bone of a Deer

The quality of sunlight. I mean the quality of light
On a morning in Iowa when you can't even remember
What you had for breakfast or even if you had
A breakfast. To float. To be young and to have broken
Free. Linden trees float above you in a lacuna
That youth has made just in time, before all of Ireland
Might have been lost to your care-worn childhood.
Coffee and the scent of cinnamon under pale leaves,
The cinnamon of Iowa City, the coffee cup
Replenished by a boy you still don't recognise as gay,
A sweetheart of a boy who misunderstood a gesture
Or a word or your ability to quote C.P. Cavafy
And all the brittle poems from a sunlit room
In Alexandria. Was Rae Delvin a boy or a girl?
How little you know of her burning, sunlit pages.
What you are thinking of is a girl with brown eyes
In a lost poem from another language, a poem
As delicate as a small boy with woman's eyes.
You are now afloat in the long American summer
After Vietnam when all of the burning issues
Became personal things. The best poets in Marvin
Bell's workshop dream of watching for fires in a forest
South-east of Seattle: they must choose, for career,
To follow Aldo Leopold's *Sand County Almanac*,
But you must choose a girl or boy fashioned from
The windswept thigh-bone of a deer. It is sunlit
Beneath these pales trees in Iowa. It is so far away
From that Irish world of wars and memoirs, from
That elderly man you knew, wearing a lemon waist-coat

And a frayed Guards tie and a scratched tank-watch
With a blue and red canvas strap. I think that man
Must have been the youth the elder loved when
He and him were very young. The housekeeper back
Home said they were both handsome but inaccessible:
I didn't know then what her tone of voice meant,
I mean her own settled and married intonation
That crackled down the line from a damp, tied cottage.
A full-size bronze of the god Hermes, a very
Expensive purchase from Artemis S.A.
Of the protector of merchants in a classical
Lysippan pose, was all the rage in the household
That summer of '78. The sculpture was
Something that defined them both, both who'd parted
Long after the housekeeper had been forsaken, and
Long before the hope of romance had returned
To Europe. That pause when Al Bowlly went silent,
Waiting for all dancers to turn and regroup
On the old vinyl that I'd rescued from among things
In a life he'd once lived, that pause of the Ray Noble Orchestra,
Seemed like the muffled 'plurp' of the Chateau
Lafite '45 his lover had brought and insisted they open.
In my life there were brilliant new openings:
This promise of sunlight in Iowa, all that cinnamon
And these coffee cups borne by persons whose names
I couldn't remember even then, but in his long life –
Ebbing away from me as our Pan-Am Jumbo
Banked in a holding pattern over Chicago, in his life
It seemed like the end of one long season
In Mayfair, the end of wine as deep as 20-year old
Tawny Port; of a deep love known once, of such
a Cru; of such a compote of Cavafy, tannin and art.

At St Gobnait's Well

Such small angels and putti to console the living and the dead:

See these offerings left at a holy well for one hundred years,
Such hope made of stone and water; and above,

On a fertile hill, that Church of Ireland rectory
Placed strategically as a bastion of old Anglicanism
In the Catholic wilds of Cùl Aodha, its timbers

Now a lattice-work opened to the heavens,
Its doors parted from hinges, a gaping rain-soaked hole

Where a bell once stood. Earth, please take no pleasure
From the disarray of this ruined honest Mission, as I take

No pleasure from faith in Gaelic poems or in a prophecy
Of holy wells, but only in time that lets all of Ireland gently down

Among angels, here where I grasp for poetry in mist and rain.

At the *Monte Carlo*, Minneapolis

to Peggy Flanagan

Peg's *Sidecar* and my *Old Fashioned* settle
In the frosted hour of this early afternoon
On a busy Monday in Minneapolis;
Busy for others, that is, the half-serious
Young men who must have come from the
Plush offices of the Wells Fargo Bank, or
Some such institute or Incorporated entity
Where young men find refuge from the very
Things we dealt with, blow by blow, as
Our twenties' cocktails succumbed to this
Greater need to not be here but to be else-
Where; to be where a guy and a gal
In a story by Scott Fitzgerald might sit and
Contemplate the continuing continuousness
Of America in the late lunch-hour. The usher
Had taken your car and parked it adroitly
In a maze of Minnesota puddles. The waitress
Who might have been the waitress
In the window of any American Hopper café,
Suspended momentarily in the hour of art,
Only coming through a tissue of time to stand
Aghast in a far distant poem, such a
Creature as holds a cigarette close in the wind:
As I was saying, there is always a waitress in
America. There is always a kindly voice to
Interrupt what you were about to say about
That day in this bar in the twenties when a

Man in a trench-coat came in. To the one
Republic, he said, as he took the day's
Takings – and to the hard-working girls, to
This town and the stories they wish to tell.

An Emergency of Ornaments

There's a crisis of excess in the world where babies
Boomed. Nobody young wants that chipped dinner

Service, nobody wants these eleven knives, 'ivories'
And genuine, made in 1958 Hong Kong; and as for

This cracked green lusterware salad bowl so full of
Yellow veins that it might be a diseased old person,

Well, there are no takers. Even a daughter's love
Or a son's pity cannot accept these yellowed veins

That now seem like diagrams from a polio epidemic
That passed away peacefully, ruining only the few

Middle-class households where children were too
Clean. This blue infrared lamp is hardly as antiseptic

As the GDR label promised. Our children want only
Travel now, bare interiors, uninterrupted sky and sea.

A Cork Fog

Let us consider this heavy fog, so quick and Elizabethan
A thing, an after-effect of last month's empire

That just passed over the brow of the hill
In a splendour of October brass. Now, even

Sunlit braids of golden thread that trailed
In the wake of musterings and leafy retreats,

Even braid, is invisible in this November fog;
And in its stead are these assemblies of grey, these

Shadows of trees like so many Viking long boats
Nudging forward in the unremarkable shallows.

Here, the Earl of Grafton fell. You heard the splash
As his efforts failed; and here, a Gael tumbled into slime

With the indecency of a cormorant as a ball from Colonel
Churchill's regiment of foot found its mark beneath fog.

That's the way it is with this heavy mist: it makes
An enemy of mere stone and it leaves chroniclers at ease –

Which is why I like to sit at this table in Electric with a stiff drink
Or two. Listen, what falls in fog is not of this world.

Sand, Ink

Toes like pens sink into the sand's ineffable quality,
And the sea in the way the sea does casts spells
And potions in the form of grain. To be exuberant
Is a terrible error at times like this, though the strand
Is an idealist, an exuberant idealist washing away
Deeper meanings; and the boat out there in the deep,
So deep and so far out in its isolated blue condition –
This boat incurs the wrath of where I stand. Let us
Call it, for the sake of truth, a personality type
Tethered only to this poem, as free-floating as ink
On sand and shell. A dissociative fugue between us.

Cruise Ship in Cork Harbour

I wave to that departing ship. I wave again
As if some part of me had gone aboard

And become a stowaway; some part of me
That's become a grey gull hitching a ride,

Some part of me that's heard a whisper
Or felt a change of wind. These gooseberries

Onshore have let me down, stripped of
Dignity by snails, hanging, serrated, careless

As wet clothes left abandoned, untidy as
Any life at home. My summer has ended

Though it's only late June. There are things
A ship can do, like bending time, like

Carrying us from summer to summer, oh,
Perpetually in full sail. Moving towards,

Moving to. There must be an Etruscan
Port or an Adriatic lagoon awaiting us, with

Snails not on these neglected gooseberries of home
But dressed and orderly on a serving dish.

Four Crew

Water rests at the catch
But your heart churns
When oars flare, your heart
Heaves and pulls
With that tall, thin boy
Of the perfect body-fat index
And a future as long as
An oar and an arm working
On water. April purrs
In a dry, cold wind
And Henley beckons
From its perch on the Thames.
The Lee shudders in its
Half-canvas of grey, no sunlight
On the time-sheet yet,
Just boys at full stretch,
Each stiffened splash
A wasted minute.
Listen to the split second
Consuming its youth. Listen.
It could have been someone else
A boy is rowing to: that girl
In a red dress, see, on the jetty,
Who waves at a purple crew,
Who longs for no one tall
Or thin, but for that fat man
In the beige panama hat
Waving too, a man beautiful
On the inside, on the inside

Tall and young. Oh, because,
She says, because, because,
You make love in a darkened room
Not a long thin shell. The show
That greets her on the wet pontoon
Has hardly anything to do with men;
A small software reading-point
As asexual as the fastest time, as
Neutral as a moon hauled in.

The Scent From Architecture

for Tess Barry

There we were in the living room of Lloyd Wright's Fallingwater,
The sound of the waters of Bear Run, the sheer aluminium
Of sunlight and the rusty burnt ochre of broadcast Fall leaves,
When a scent like a scent I hadn't sensed in years came in on
The autumn wind and settled in the space that you now occupied
On the waxed flagstone floor between an Edgar Kaufmann
Portrait by Victor Hammer and Edgar's Danish vase by Axel Salto.
The scent had a top note of citrus and peach. There was thyme
And pine needle, there was Pittsburgh and fashion and the 1930s and
All of nature in a tadelakt slip-case. In life scent is visual and love's best
Ambiance, by far, is indirect, as Frank Lloyd Wright's lightest
Gesture was to send a cantilevered floor out over the Pennsylvania
Woods to collect what was wild and astringent in American life –
Such notes settling around us now, such oak-moss, citrus, vetiver.

A Celtic Miscellany

Magic rain magic mist magic dew magic hail
Magic darkness magic sea magic waves magic
River magic fountain magic well magic spring
That bursts forth when a magic spear pierces
Rock magic oak tree magic ash magic lime tree
Magic bough magic yew magic hawthorn magic
Tree to make you young again magic tree to
Prevent hunger magic thorn magic ivy magic
Fern magic blossom, mistletoe and mandrake
Magic sallie rod magic wheat magic breath
Magic blood magic feather magic dung magic
Piss magic mantle magic trousers magic veil
Magic hat magic chain magic sword magic
Shield magic hearth magic bench magic door
Magic cry of a deer or cry of a magic deer;
Seven as a magic number magic the human
Head for divination magic also the head of
A dog, magic too vessels that burst in the fire
To uncover dis-obedience magic the river
That rises to drown liars magic the stone
That causes deafness magic the deep lake
That causes forgetfulness magic the hazel-nut
That makes a lover foolish magic the stone
That banishes sorrow magic the charm bought
Cheaply in the form of small poetry books,
Or nine the magic number and again the magic
Number seven and the magic twelve also,
And green as that magic colour dye as magic
Red as magic black as magic white as magic

Purple also as a magic hue and also red again;
Magic also the felling of two trees in a wood
And the magic wand used by the Druids to
Find your beloved carried away by fairies –
And, when all else fails, magic the new fangled
Blessings of Christians swarming into our oak
Wood, making even the disappeared speak.

Last Flight

in memory of Molly Keane

It's a foolish old bird that mistakes an open window for water,
But this bird has just committed a fatal error

And become for as long as you care to look at it
A shredded canvas by Morris Graves, a spirit bird

Out of the monochrome fifties where even the sea
And the seashore of Ardmore bay makes a perfect wash

For a blackbird's last flight. She settled here like a bird
Already wounded, down to her last case of peach champagne,

Re-stitching her damaged feathers the way she stitched
Again the damaged fire-screen that was a wedding-present

From Mrs Astaire. And Mrs Astaire's son, Fred,
That gentle, too-thin boy who gave her an iron-bench

Made to order by the blacksmith in Lismore, this Fred
I've just seen again dancing with Eleanor Powell:

Such synchronous spirit birds, such characters from a book
Where humans move perfectly, such chapters of grace

That everything we write seems amateurish, unlovely, as open
To crisis as any blackbird, unlike anything of 'Begin the Beguine'.

Vermeer and Thrift

I've been howling like a fool about these few Euro
In my pocket. With Vermeer it was always an appearance.
It was a lady observing herself, deviating just a little
From the lady before a mirror in Frans van Mieris.
How they could compress the deepest effects of art
Into the smallest space possible, that's what annoys me –
As an Irishman, I mean, with my three dull colours
Jingling in my pocket. Gabriel Metsu who painted
No fewer than sixteen scenes with music has kept
His mouth shut for four hundred years. I am provoked
By his embarrassment of riches, such pride
Kept hidden offends me. My offense is so dolorous,
So Catholic that I am dying with the Bourbon kings.
Caspar Netscher's duet at the virginal is so refined
It hides all of Holland, or it compresses our view
Of history through a solid door-frame, a '*doorkikje*',
As if wealth was an interior without humans. Please
Keep your pride secret, like Samuel van Hoogstraten
Who leads our gaze into the depth: in life as in
Politics we are looking in upon a suite of rooms. And
This other Dutch fellow, this Jan Steen, his bare-
Faced cheek is unbelievable. Not for him the broom
Against a door jamb, the slippers, the keys in a lock,
But the skull and lute. Come again, I whisper
To his artwork in a frame, come again. Tell us of
Vanitas objects. Tell us that tax havens are transient.

'Adam et Eve' by Francis Picabia

If Picasso was God then you were a true non-believer,
The one who made art not-art, the one who became
Obsessed with an iconography of games of chance,
Knowing that our heads are made round so that we may
Change direction, or have no direction, like this grand
And formal portrait, this almost erotic photograph in
Paint where Eve has a belly-button and an orchid,
All dominant in pink and brown for the private parts
That may be Adam's destination. Or perhaps not –
In truth, Adam does look like someone's boyfriend,
But not Eve's. The years you painted this, almost a
Photograph out of *Paris Plaisir*, your smooth, uncanny
Skin tones, your lascivious brushstrokes, were the years
Your daughter recruited Beckett into a Resistance unit,
Gloria SMH. You had enlisted the machinery of the world
For private art while she had changed direction in a way
That could never be art, but could be, instead, tiny dots
Of ink hidden inside cigarettes. A father almost a Fascist
Protects a daughter inside history. So perfectly God-like.

The Seven Pear Trees of Avigdor Arikha

Not rest, but arrest. This iron foundry
Where I work, this place they call art
Is where I slave in a frenzy of prayer.
If time covers me with the comfort of
An Anglo-Irish chinchilla rug
It is a vintage car not an armchair
That my unhappy arms now rest upon;

And if I seem merely a gorgeous
Throwback to another era in fine art,
It is not Samuel Beckett's fault
Or the fault of any man who stays
Awake, who cannot sleep with all
The fuss injustice makes.
Pastel and paint will pay for this in days

And days of busier furnaces offstage –
My incomparable grasp of the past
Is no more real than seven pears in a tree;
Nor can the fountain, pitcher, fruit, assuage
Acuity of vision in a Mogilev foundry.
This basket of iron fruit can't possibly last
As pears on glass, as transcendent dust.

Last Service in the Orthodox Synagogue

for Simon Lewis

It was a soft day in Israel and more than a last Shabbat
When all the published pages of young David Marcus came apart

And fell again as vellum droplets of Cork rain. I looked
Back with undiminished love at the quires David made –

Even the last wet moon wore the courtesy of a yarmulka.
It's not that our days have been young and fiery, but this day

Was as old as the seams on Maurice Hurwitz's fawn coat.
Maurice, I miss you. But you would surely have come

With me. We might have been alone together the way
Friends can halve a lonely apartness, that feeling after

You've had to hide who you are. A London Rabbi told you how
They had machines beyond Ireland, new machines for killing Jews.

'Ah, Europe, the end of our beginning', your father said.
You sing 'The Banks of My Own Lovely Lee' in Hebrew as all shuffle

Through the door. Your scrolls will be sent elsewhere; there will be
Nobody left to remember. As Cork's barley-sugar melts in my pocket

I cross the iron bridge that was named by Mayor Goldberg and think,
Again, how this disturbed world still has important negative

Consequences for Jews. Ah, look here, grey rain for relief; the soft
Cork rain that fell for a century upon uncollated Jewish quires.

The Voice of Larry Cunningham

I left these last Seniors, some put down for Princeton
And the East, with an image of Becket and his father
Striding among the Wicklow hills, the grainy image
Of swirling mist and spectral great-coats a metaphor
Surely of the impossibility of connections, as
Impossible an image as a poet like Desmond O'Grady
Who strode through Tipperary town only to rest
Awhile in the drawing room scene of Fellini's
La Dolca Vita. There are ungraded essays on my desk
Of sturdy old Dungarvan oak, essays now redundant
As my grades are settled upon these gifted youths,
As settled as the dust settled on a pretty little girl
From Omagh who came outdoors at the wrong
Moment in Irish historical studies, her broken neck
As broken as the saddest character in John McGahern's
Lovely Leitrim. I had held a green umbrella aloft
While something orgasmic happened in Irish Studies
And I've come indoors from the heat of a late April
University campus to play with spools, old tapes and
Voices I captured from a time when I was neither
Coming nor going, but merely surviving in a world
I'd made bearable with a second-hand tape-machine
Bought in Frank Sweeney's shop; surviving, I remember
Now, when I had no connections whatsoever, no
Connection with any human on this earth, for music
Had failed me in that world beyond small tapes
And their capacity to be overwritten with re-
Edited memories: but I never over-wrote the tape

With his golden voice, a voice as resonant as
The burnished wood of a viola, a voice that promised
Me that if only I developed a tone, even singing to
Myself, I'd be perfectly at home in any Tipperary town.

Majestic

I didn't mean to stay in the Majestic at Harrogate
As if it was just a festive day in 1954, especially
Now that your telephonic message has reached me
To say that you are in the Palace bar in Torquay
And warmer by several degrees. A different sea
Calls to you and you say it is never too late
To take a dip at noon, particularly now that a waiter
From Clacton has offered you a swimming lesson,
You fortified with three Manhattans, and he, the
Scoundrel, having won medals in the breaststroke, crawl,
And other contortions of the human frame. It may be,
My love, Guy Lombardo's tripping 'Blue Skirt Waltz'
That has gone to your head, but that other sound
I imagine, that fellow's 'The Moon of Manakoora',
Will fling you into any old stranger's eager arms;
And I fear the worst from music, as I always have.
This veranda is a prison without you, this ground
With all its grandiose June foliage is all the poorer
For my having missed you, yet again. Such charms
As the journey had are long gone, and the Supergrid
With its giant transformers and tons of insulation
Impresses me less and less. You have caught the
Frantic atmosphere of England, you have. You
Want to taste everything while it's British and new.
Even bungalows impress you. The platform at Crewe
Stole your heart, the Lyon's tea-room, the queue
At Boot's waiting for their books, this new version
Of life that teems with life, this life unlike the heap
Of turf we left behind in Ireland. This voltage
You feel needs twelve tons of craft-paper, it needs

An orderly step-down, it needs at least a four mile
Run across an empty airfield. Will England ever empty
Out like Ireland has, or will it always be full of skiffle
In smoke-filled basements; in the Majestic where
I am trapped with myself only, or down in Torquay
Where all the men who have limbs left on them
After the war want to go swimming with your long
Red hair, not to mention your long-distance running
Legs. Life isn't fair. Here I am a fully qualified half
Decent engineer sitting on the veranda of the Majestic
With my Irish nurse gone swimming. And I know
I've lost you from this purring of the new English grid.

In Reduced Circumstances

In these dark days, the way things are, even ghosts
Must live in reduced circumstances. The land has
Run out of wax for candles. There is hardly enough
Light to read the long appendices of the hanged.
You couldn't put a name on the odd ghost you'd
See with a stretched neck and a hard-luck story.
It was the land made him turn again to sheep
Stealing in the fields above Macroom, and it was
The bad influence of a drinking-companion made
Him take the seven greenish tablecloths from the
Bishop's palace; the Catholic bishop, he explained,
The one who was really in with God. This town-
Land and this landscape is really at the fag-end
Of an era of excuses. Here are my dead friends,
Sheep-stealers and vagabonds, poachers; and poets
So full of the names of the hanged – Mr Riordan,
The journeyman-tailor who entered into combinations,
John Rohan who killed Abigail Kennedy, Denis, John
And Patrick Regan, for highway robbery and assault,
Not to mention Mick Rourke whose ghost still drifts
Over the North Infirmary dissection room; Mr Ryall
Of Doneraile whose crime went with a craving for
Food, the utter prostration of the human spirit in
A time of great want – so full of the hanged, these
Poets, as I was saying, you'd almost think that verse
Was a thing made up instead of something merely
Remembered and terrible. Whereas we know from
The curate who fled, one Francis Sylvester Mahony,
That memory is merely the Attic salt in a Celtic

Realm, that Horace and Pliny may have classic
Things to teach us, but their books still smell, here,
Of turf-smoke and persistent rain. Thank you,
Father Prout, for still remaining obscure. You
Give us courage, you make us want to go on
Writing to ourselves, or writing just to you as
You quaff another Orvieto or a whacker and glass
Of Hewitt's best distilled. It is true, as you
Reported in Dicken's *Globe*, that the Vatican
Banned stethoscopes and railways: that something
As intimate as a heart murmur should only be
Heard by God and something as evil as a train
Should never be heard in a field. You have to
Hand it to them, Father, century after century
These holy idiots grow holier still. As for me, I
Can only perceive such ghosts in the landscape
And how they mingle with the sweetest memories
From my own life – of my own wife, for instance,
A girl you'd run away with as soon as the first
Candle was lit; thinking like a memory from Rome
Of how perfect she looked under chestnut trees
That seemed as smug as ghosts; thinking what
Love can do to haunted landscapes we live within;
Of the yearning for restrictions around us, the
Constant fear of breaching someone's etiquette,
Of how we love in these ghosts and metaphors,
Though love, as you know, was never used in Cork
Until a day we dropped two lovers on a scaffold.

At Thoor Ballylee

If we could only find some personal conviction
In ourselves, not be as dispirited as a heavy soil
Or as inevitable as a tree; as unlearned as
An attitude of our fathers. If this heavy rain,
Which is really only vapours off the boil
And growing cold in Co. Galway, if this rain has
Any meaning other than itself, then a stain

Or Yeatsean watermark should be
Impressed upon us here. This slate roof
Should give us back more than an
Echo of rain. I should really be able to see
A sign, maybe an impression of a horse's hoof
Where a huntsman rode by, or a window frame
Filled with ghostly senators. But these trees

And their April leaves are all that's left
For me. The spirits of the place are elsewhere,
Maybe thousands of miles away in
Villanova or Princeton. This tower is bereft
Of an intellectual life. This empty seminar
Of rain and late floods makes it plain
That a theft happened here, a grand theft.

I wonder is there anything broken that I
Might restore again? The unwritten page.
As you know, still thirsts and thirsts for
Accusations. Where the gods lie
Is where these trees explode in a rage
Of small April leaves. If only we could pour
Our hearts out without irony in this country.

Guy Lombardo

But it begins again when listening to Guy Lombardo
And his Royal Canadians. Out of the depth or height
Of a summer barbecue in Ontario, everywhere I look,
Sunshine follows me as if 'I don't want to walk without you'
Or 'South of the Border' leads to a kind of July
That turns up the orange glow of a late afternoon.
It's just that a familiar kind of warmth, warm irregular
Stones of your Glenshelane patio, our two glasses with
Dried crimson flakes of old sherry, this patio that
Seemed like a small country for making poems, this
Space between me and fragments of shrimp-pink
Petals shearing away from Violet Carson, followed by
Great clusters of Paddy McGredy, Super Star's vermilion,
The velvet purse of tight Papa Meilland, the indecisive
Depth of yellow fringe of pink in Peace; it's just that
Something settled in Ontario long ago, a patio as
Small as Ulster, a tiny place with planters or pioneers,
Like the small Protestant note in Irish history that you
Have claimed to hear since childhood. You have heard
It, you said, over and over, and you are as content with
This as any patriot in a foreign jail. For me, it was not
A country or a province, but more an afterglow, as subtle
As the subtle bouquet-garni or the rare essence of
Rose petals; all so like pollen it would make you dizzy.
Because I, like you, must always remain true to my heart
I admit I saw the green and the yolk of Ireland part,
Never to be made whole again, never in all Balmoral
Seasons. And not to declare this is a kind of treason:
I am as odd as be-damned. I am of no historical use

To anyone who doesn't have roses to prune. For my
One true companion I summon up dear Fr Prout,
That Catholic loyalist in his two-volume Regina edition:
Father, it's too late to stop O'Connell. The die is
cast, and wildly, the way O'Connell's Repealers flung
Fresh vegetables of a Dingle bible colony into the sea
at Inch. What was orange clung to the rocks, wouldn't
give way. Somewhere a Huguenot called to me from
The depths, from a Canton under the sea. Nobody heard.
But I heard: another kind of history entered my head
With its cracked green shell, its one toppled Omphalos.

Taking Instructions from Gertrude Jekyll

A woodland at its best is only wallpaper, as death
Is also a kind of membrane, moist but stiffening
When the year turns. It is summer when we pass
Along the borders, but there are white foxgloves
At the edge of a beech wood. Between us and the time
It takes to walk into autumn there's a mass
Of leaves, leaves trodden down close, and all
The mould that hides our last Alstroemerias.
Let me tell you when the fern-walk is at its best;
I mean late August, of course, in a damp wood
Where you must always remember the dead.
Quite simply, only those who can truly remember
Can see our true companions, Linnaea, Trientalis
And Trillium – they have a burned nature of wood.
They fold into us like mothers at a coffin, like
Sisters still turning over the neat habits of growth
In the hope of finding the disappeared; of turning
Suddenly into a copse of half-hardy Helichrysum
Or Tritomas with their doubtful endurance.
The wet sky has a green wash. Even at night
When you walk here the moon works lightly with
Its silver adjustments, making the stems of holly
Into legs of deer frozen to earth in fear; here
Where the fox has cantered, as pictorial
As the moods of autumn, as beautiful
As the long ridge of dwarf Andromeda.
I wish I could tell you when the night stories began
Of the small bush roses that make no use
Of moonlight or limping deer, or impish foxes

Rustling between sempervirens and lavender.
When it's moist you should remember the touch of
Something light and green: time itself, I think –
Let me tell you again, all the moist spaces in your life
Should be filled with wet marigolds, with zinnias.

Acknowledgements

Thanks to the following magazines, journals and digital magazines who first published the work here: *Agenda*, *Irish Examiner*, *Irish Times*, *PN Review*, *Poetry* (Chicago), *Poetry Review*, *Cyphers*, *Poetry Ireland Review*, *Poetry Encounters*, *Plume Poetry*. 'Garden of Remembrance' was first published as part of a commission by the Irish Writers' Centre, Dublin. Grateful acknowledgement is made to the Arts Council of Ireland for their continuing support through Aosdána. Thanks are also due to the Munster Literature Centre, Cork, and its director, poet Patrick Cotter, for support and encouragement over the years.